Long Distance

Bilingual Press/Editorial Bilingüe
Canto Cosas

Series Editor
Francisco Aragón

Publisher
Gary D. Keller

Executive Editor
Karen S. Van Hooft

Associate Editors
Adriana M. Brady
Brian Ellis Cassity
Amy K. Phillips
Linda K. St. George

Address
Bilingual Press
Hispanic Research Center
Arizona State University
PO Box 875303
Tempe, Arizona 85287-5303
(480) 965-3867

Long Distance

poems by steven cordova

Bilingual Press/Editorial Bilingüe
Tempe, Arizona

Library of Congress Cataloging-in-Publication Data

Cordova, Steven.
    Long distance / Steven Cordova.
        p. cm. – (Canto Cosas)
    ISBN 978-1-931010-62-7 (pbk. : alk. paper)
    1. AIDS (Disease)–Patients–Poetry. 2 Gay men–New York (State)–New York–Poetry. I. Title.
    PS3603.O73425L66 2009
    811'.6–dc22

                                       2009030795

PRINTED IN THE UNITED STATES OF AMERICA

Front cover art: Herido *(1992–93) by Miguel Ángel Reyes*

Cover and interior design by Bill Greaves, Concept West

Acknowledgments are on pp. xi–xii.

Canto Cosas

Funded in part by grants from the National Endowment for the Arts and the Arizona Commission on the Arts, this new series is designed to give further exposure to Latina and Latino poets who have achieved a significant level of critical recognition through individual chapbooks and publication in periodicals or anthologies or both, but who have not necessarily had their own books of poetry published. Under the watchful eye of series editor, poet, and small press publisher Francisco Aragón, the books in Canto Cosas aim to reflect the aesthetic diversity in American poetry. There are no restrictions on ethnicity, nationality, philosophy, ideology, or language; we will simply continue our commitment to producing high-quality poetry. The books in this series will also feature introductions by more established voices in the field.

for Simon

Contents

I

II

Acknowledgments

Many thanks to the editors of the following publications where some of these poems first appeared:

A&U: "The Next Generation"

Barrow Street: "Across a Table" ("I'm glad you're positive")

Borderlands: "Sissy Boy"

BorderSenses: "The Last AIDS Cat"

Cimarron Review: "Punched"

The Cortland Review: "Testing Positive"

Dánta: "Driving Toward Lake Superior," "At the Delacorte," "Club St. Vitus Male Dancer"

Diner: "Meditations on the Jordaan," "Meditations on Three Men," "Ms. Daydream to You"

Evergreen Chronicles: "Loose Change"

Gertrude: "Long Distance"

The Journal: "Pecking Orders"

La Petite Zine: "That Big Noise," "Late Nineties Noir," "The Chicken and the Egg Having Sex"

Lodestar Quarterly: "Choking Victim," "Drinking Buddies"

Northwest Review: "The Next Right Thing" (as "Of Sorts"), "In Your Defense"

Zone 3: "At the North Sea"

"Now" appeared in *Ravishing DisUnities: Real Ghazals in English*, Agha Shahid Ali, ed. (Wesleyan University Press, 2000).

"Revenant Image," "The Next Right Thing" (as "Of Sorts"), "Sissy Boy," "The Next Generation," "In Your Defense," "Lullaby," "Poem for a Friend Troubled by Noise," "Two Nocturnes," both of the poems entitled "Across a Table," "Loose Change," "Club St. Vitus Dancer," "That Big Noise" (as

"Courting Fear"), "Driving Toward Lake Superior," "At the Delacorte," and "Now" appeared in my chapbook *Slow Dissolve* (Momotombo Press, 2003).

"Across a Table" ("I'm glad you're positive") also appeared in *Best Gay Poetry 2008* (A Midsummer Night's Press, 2008).

Speaking of the Living

Alberto Ríos

These poems are as hard to put down as they are to read. Full of humor and love and worry, these simple lines are the singular telling of a life shadowed by an HIV-positive diagnosis. But make no mistake: they are the telling of a life first, a life that shows itself in its complexity every step of the way. And even more than that, the poems make us want to come along.

These are intimate not in that they share particularly intimate detail, but in that they don't try to force any kind of detail onto the reader beyond the normal, the regular, the everyday—this is an inordinately greater intimacy, trusting the reader to stick with the poems once the premium of expectation has worn off. This is not Christmas day or Valentine's Day or some anniversary or other—this is a book filled by one life constructed as a whole, and that wholeness is both this book's heart and brain. It simply offers itself in its every day.

Sometimes that day is big and given to feeling, telling "How somewhere one thing is always eclipsing another, body / passing between sun and planet, dream between him & / him & him," or "The universe at times is simply that which lies / above...."

Reverie, however, is just as often matched with pragmatism, as when the speaker offers himself to another in this way: "Search the world—I'll feed your lovebirds / & your cats...." It may not be much at first blush, but the offer frees both parties in that moment, one to wander freely and one to stop wandering but with a purpose, while both find a curious common ground in wandering, both speak the same language of understanding, though perhaps at first laughing at the seeming disconnection. You go that way and I'll go this way, the poem says, but we're both in search of something—and that is the connection.

And the humor.

Humor is the sweet and sour sauce of this book. But what is the humor in AIDS? There may be none, but the life lived is still alive, and humor is a big part of that life, as we are shown many times. Hard as it is—hard, rather than hard-edged—the humor here is insightful in the sense of humanizing this particular journey. Some of the humor is ready enough—in "13 Things to Do Once I'm Dead," for example, and beyond the title itself, the poet lists "Bill myself as an underground artist." The moment is immediately extended in the next item, "Claim I stand just under 6'." The artfulness of these assertions and this humor, however, leads from the immediate to the resonant "Make every day Day of the Dead." A line like that speaks of the living as much as the dead, the narrator looking in the mirror as much as writing to someone else. And in the moment we laugh, we are connected to the speaker.

It is odd to think that HIV-positive stories might already be filled with old bromides, but popular culture moves very quickly, so that what's new in the morning is already chided by the afternoon. HIV-positive discourses are reasonably new to the world and yet are so often tiresome in a pop-culture timeframe. These poems move beyond this narrowing trap, learning instead from what is already a generational understanding, and moving toward a sense of "next," bringing the reader in tow. In often easy conversational tones, the poems speak to a dailiness that is not pop culture entertainment but rather pop culture's real life.

Indeed, in these poems popular culture is a character every bit as much as the narrator is, everything from *Star Trek*—and indeed a very particular later *Star Trek* series—to Spencer Tunick's contemporary photographing of the grandly naked spirit. The embrace of this outward life stands in contrast to its insides, to the very personal imaginings of the narrator, who lives both lives. The situation is reconciled, however, with both wit and wisdom: "With dreams we can be in two places." And at the core, outside or inside, the engine is the same: "At work I eat lunch / & surf the Web, check my e-mail first / & last for love."

As I said at the beginning, these poems are as hard to put down as they are hard to read. They are difficult because they gift us with an understanding of this life, at least for the moments we visit through these pages. And in these moments, even the smallest things begin to make sense: "How we police the edges—hair cutting, fingernail-clipping. . . . / Or how it all gets away from us. . . ."

These are poems from the middle, where the real news is, and that is their edge. They find lives and not numbers, voices and not statistics, humor and not its exhaustion. This is not to say that the poems ignore an underlying truth, not ever, but they move forward instead of standing still. They act more than think. Illness is just one part of this life, along with eating and laughing and generally just looking around at the world. What makes these poems new in their way is their unvarnished straightforwardness in living this perspective, their voyaging insistence, their drive forward, even with so many stop signs. Forward.

Toward answers. But what are the answers? In these poems, and in this life, the narrator reports on how the talk of medicines "polysyllablizes" information. That, of course, is the stuff of nonanswers struggling to sound like answers. The alternative, however, may or may not be any better: "Hoping / the more friction (fiction?) we made, // the more we'd keep it away. . . ." The search goes on, and these pages are a help, but no single answer satisfies or completes either the narrator or the reader. The moment we as readers recognize that, we are in this together with the narrator.

Don't look for self-pity in these poems, though you will find some. Don't look for answers, though the book is full of them, unsatisfying as they may sometimes be. Don't look for sadness, though you will walk on its sovereign ground. Look for the man. Look for the life.

Loose Change

Search the world—I'll feed your lovebirds
& your cats: young Dinah, old Celia.

"Need more bird feed?" your note reads,
"Fish for the quarters in my penny jar."

I do & I come up with more than the occasional
quarter. There's a nickel, a dime, a matchbook

with a scribbled name & number—stars in a brown cauldron.
An expired license gasps

for light. You look harried in the shot,
just back from overseas. Thus these foreign tokens—

little monuments to dead kings & queens.
Just days after you left (this time), Barry found himself

in the glare of a hospital bed, leaving me
the sole charge of five cats, two birds—

Barry places penny jars throughout his rooms,
trails of crumbs. In cases of lost fortune

or a ginger brush with death,
we think ourselves too old for piggy banks

& fairy tales. My mother has told one story
a thousand times: on frequent whims her father swept in

from his store to unleash a storm of pennies.
She & her two sisters happily knelt

to earn an allowance from the floor.
I gather loose change, return it to your collection

in a series of dull clinks. A young Dinah Washington croons
on compact disc. Celia sounds like cielo, Spanish

for "heaven"—"the heavens." You want a lover. Barry wants
to be well. I want to be free

of want. Entering an unlit room, I bump
a dresser. A jar rattles. Two birds sing.

The Next Generation

the New York Marble Cemetery,
2nd Street between 1st & 2nd Avenues

We wake early—
3:00, 4:00, 5:00 a.m.,
can't go back to sleep.
James lives off FDR
where roads, sidewalks,
desire lines, lie quiet.
Tom hopes to find another
livelihood, but arranges flowers
in an outdoor shop. I set
five pills upon a stand:
one a lily-white diamond;
one a capsule half-buttercup,
half-rust; the remaining three
bachelor-button blue, oblong.
I must take four of five with food;
a piece of bread sits among them,
a glass of water, and sometimes,
a book of poems I'll read
if work is light today.
My necktie slows the time
it takes to swallow. Still-lifes.
Arrangements. Keeping
current. So many things
take time: Tom waves
away a wasp; James
finds a bench to sit
and read; these pills take time:
Billy, Roger, Dallas . . .
died without them.

Someone erects an easel
to paint a portrait of James
on his bench. Tom decides
this vase is done, finished.
Outside my bedroom window
there's a small cemetery
with many trees. Twigs
cross-hatch the sky. Leaves
escort a breeze. I hear clucks,
crows (a neighbor keeps
chickens, roosters).
A bachelor-button blue
slips into my bath:
the pigment of a slow dissolve.

It's Always the Same on Star Trek

A Borg ship crosses paths
with the Federation starship *Voyager*—
the lovely-in-middle-age Captain Katherine Janeway
in command—& the Borg—in a calm, masculine voice—
ask the *Voyager* crew to lower ship shields
& surrender. "We will add your biological
& technological distinctiveness to our own.
Your culture
          will adapt
                  to service us.
Resistance is futile." It's hard to love
a Borg: one real eye, one red beam-projecting sensor
where the other eye should be; one real
& one robotic arm—black, metal, threatening.
Worst of all, the Borg possess the fashion sense
of a gay man "into leather." (It is unclear, however,
whether Borg drones have sex at all.) Still,
Captain Janeway tortures herself
when forced to destroy a Borg ship:
Oh, for before any Borg is a Borg
he or she is a member of one of the thousands
of advanced cultures assimilated by
the even more advanced Borg.
What then are we to make of the Borg episodes?
Clearly, the Borg automatons are antagonists.
But they can also hear each other's thoughts
& they are lonely when "liberated"
from "the hive mind."
I believe the Borg episodes
are about class, that they serve
as a warning against the bliss

of servitude. *Your culture*

                    will adapt

                                      to service us—

Oh, no, not for Captain Janeway
& her commanding officers as they fly off—
on top once again—penetrating the deep recesses
of space at warp speed 9. . . .

Even in the 24th century it seems it's better
to be
       & be served
than to be a drone, a worker-bee among the stars,
happy with universal health care, lots of friends
& something like understanding.

Long Distance

Now that you're back home
you're trying, you say, to "stay
with" the laundry. I don't ask
what exactly that means. I know:

before you came to live with me you'd given up
on laundry. Then, turning over a new leaf
of fabric softener, you befriended Annie,
the old New Yorker—white, white-haired
and short—who mans the corner 'mat.
Weekdays she showed you when to pour,
how to count American change.
You bought her a muffin from the corner café
where the attractive wait-staff took to waving
at us in passing, calling out to you
by name, "Sigh-men, Sigh-men."
Weekends we folded by that cavernous dryer,
you know the one—you can see the blue tips
of flames whenever Annie folds down its top.
We made a show of kissing each time corners
brought us arm to open arm, chest to chest.

Crawling into bed last night
you lifted the sheet, held it
to your sweet and blushing face.
"Does it smell fresh?" I asked,
then woke before you answered.

Posing Nude for Spencer Tunick

I decided not to primp much the night before. In the morning,
I shaved around my Vandyke, unusual for me on a Saturday,
trimmed my graying chest hair. Here & there I plucked at a
shoulder. The apartment was cold at 6 a.m. But the bath water
ran warm & I'd had a good night's sleep.

Steve called just before I switched off the bedside lamp.

He'd been busy & had almost gone home without reading his
e-mail. "I don't know if I have the guts to do this alone,"
I'd typed, "but if you come with. . . ." Waiting for Steve to
respond, I'd surprised myself. I'd resolved, more or less, to do it
on my own. Then Steve was on the phone, in the nick, saying
he'd meet me at the designated spot.

*

It's always colder, windier on the Hudson—a fact I forgot in
my hurry to be in the Meatpacking District by 7:30. In jeans,
a T-shirt & a gray thermal, I'm underdressed. I spot an
acquaintance or two, smoking & chatting outside the restaurant
Florent. I say hello to the welcome wagon & check in.

*

Steve is seated on a leather-padded bench running along the east
wall. Along the west wall, there's a bar & a row of stools. The
restaurant chairs & tables have been cleared & about 100
men—& a handful of women—mill about, yawning or scanning
the room for a friendly face. Some sip coffee from paper cups.

*

He looks small—Steve does—sitting on the bench gone bulky
with coats, small beneath his own gray jacket. In a minute, he'll
rise & kiss the back of my neck.

In a minute I'll lean back into him.

*

One of Tunick's assistants asks us to remove our jewelry. One of
my rings jams & heading for the bathroom for soap & water, I
hear Florent say, "I've never been naked in my own restaurant
before."

*

A middle-aged woman, bleached blond, lifts her hair to show
Steve & me the Crixivan hump on her back. "I'm embarrassed
by it," she admits. Steve responds quickly, "It's not noticeable
with your hair down." I say, "Plus it isn't anything to be
ashamed of." And the feeling of inadequacy that washes over us
has nothing to do with the fact that we're all naked.

*

Tunick and his tripod are perched on a table, and he gets riled
each time one of his assistants, who I think is cute, bumps into it.
The assistant bumps into it. Tunick snaps. The assistant blushes.

Tunick is an ordinary-looking man who charms with his ability
to articulate. He smiles when he's speaking to the assembled
nudity. He smiles & articulates. He creates a sense of
camaraderie.

*

A man raises his hand & asks whether the HIV-negative are welcome. Tunick responds diplomatically that he'll take their picture later. The inquiring man & a handful around him gather their clothes & as they're leaving the center of the room, someone says, "For once, they're the ones being rejected."

*

Tunick's mantra for avoiding closed eyes in his pictures is "One, close your eyes. Two, open them. Three, keep them open." I breathe between one & two. Try to relax my face just before three.

*

The whole room laughs when Tunick, adjusting the shot, says, "You, with the shaved head, close your legs." "You, kneel." Or "You, relax your belly." I'd like to think I was like butter, but Steve says I was leaning so hard against the picture on the wall, he thought I'd bring it down.

*

Between shots I spot someone I knew, though not well, during the ACT UP heyday. Ten-plus years later, I still see him. Usually on a downtown street. He is always warm when we stop to chat. And there he is now, hands cupped over his own genitals. Overwhelmed by what I want, by what I've always wanted, I look away.

"Hold on," I say to Steve once I have my clothes back on. And I go in search of my old ACT UP fantasy.

"I didn't want to leave without saying hello to you—& giving you a kiss."

"I saw you," he says, pulling his lips away from mine, his smile bold and self-conscious all at the same time. And I say it, too. I say, "I saw you, too."

*

One, two . . . open. Three . . . keep them open.

*

Steve & I decide not to eat at Florent. It will be a while before Tunick's equipment is broken down & everything is back to the way it was before. Hungry & searching for a restaurant he once ate at, Steve & I are leaning into one another at a crossroads just west of Hudson, giggling like club-goers who've been up all night. It's still early & there's not a soul about, no one but us stepping over the chipped & sinking cobblestones.

Having been someone else's medium for a while, we cross Hudson.

13 Things to Do Once I'm Dead

1. Stop thinking about death.

2. Crank up The Dead; befriend Deadheads.

3. Read: "The Dead," *The Naked
    and the Dead*, *Death Comes
    for the Archbishop*, *As I Lay
    Dying*, *The Death of the Heart*,
    and *A Handful of Dust*.

4. Bill myself as an underground artist.

5. Claim I stand just under 6'.

6. Come to a Dead End.

7. On those rare occasions when something the living say or do
    shocks, roll over in my grave.

8. Mean what I say, even when what I mean and what I say is
    nothing.

9. Die in death as many deaths as I died in life.

10. Study a language, any language, so long as it's dead.

11. Place a classified ad. "Wanted—
    Tall, Handsome Grave Robber,
    No Experience Necessary. I will train him."

12. Make every day Day of the Dead.

13. Open a vacation spot,
    call it Death Valley
    or Dead Sea Bed
    & Breakfast. (Vacancies,
    a neon sign will blink.
    Vacancies. Vacancies.)

Across a Table

Talk between us
flows, finally,

on the subject of regimens,
yours, mine, drugs

with names like the names
of second-rate Greek gods. We begin

with mine: Protease
inhibitor Nelfinavir. Stavudine, Lamivudine.

Talk between us, sesquipedalian, rhymes, polysyllablizes,
civilizes, even,

the raw need that wafts over
cooked food that brings us—two strangers—here together

across a table.
Now yours, which, I'm sorry, runs

together in my mind: VidexVireadSustiva-
CombivirCrixivan.

And now the litany
of side effects: hump-back-nausea-neuropathy-

need-for-hip-replacement-
heart-disease.

The candle, the moon—
centerpiece, centerpiece—

are going down. Protease stands over
a decapitated Medusa

and yet we sit, you and I,
silent as stone and stone.

Choking Victim

who waits for you across a table, hands at his own throat,

who shook your hand once, who threw in a "Nice to meet you,"

who couldn't speak to you, not now, not even if he wanted to,

who folds in your embrace & spits it up, spits it all up,

who leaves you with a partially masticated piece of fowl

    and the restaurant's fading applause,

who, back at his plate, laughs and carries on like nothing

    happened between you, nothing at all,

who leans to his left to whisper in the ear of the prime, the more

    perfect choice seated to his right,

who shakes your hand, "Good night," assures you, "We'll do

    lunch sometime,"

who, while he was choking, teared, his tears

    shining like the medal you hoped he'd hang about your neck.

Drinking Buddies

My last ten buys us the first round, your credit
the second, the third. . . . You're young. You hold
your liquor well. I'm just turned 40
with little in my stomach. Come 9:40
you stand, drunkenly sign the credit
slip, then high-tail it to a phone. "Hold

on," you're saying, "my wife won't mind I'm out
late"—not since you're only out with me.
I ponder the naïve nature of that trust
sitting here on this stool I've come to trust.
I'm out as queer. Tonight we're out
together. And are you safe? Are you safe with me?

The bartender doesn't seem to mind
my gay-speak or my smile. So I'd say yes
on that count. And I'll confess I just checked out your ass
but like you too much to make an ass
of myself. I hope that you don't mind,
that when you read this we'll still be friends. Yes?

Late-Nineties Noir

One night, after a downfall, I saw these fireflies
in the New York Marble, hovering over the markers
& beneath the trees, lined up, side by side, like pallbearers.
Some guys got a view of Central Park, the Empire State.
Me—I got a view of the New York Marble Cemetery.
One night, one downfall of his own, he saw them too.

We used to kiss—him, me—hard, so hard
his eyes rolled back, green into the dark
of his head. Afterward, we'd talk,
talk about the one-eyed green fireflies.
I'd try to get at what he did
& he said he found stuff

& put it together in pictures.
Baggy army pants & a white V-neck tee—
that's what he wore & he wore it until it was see-through.
His blond mop was always cropped, though,
& even if it was only 25 bucks he forked over
once a year to a city gym, he forked it over—

smooth mounds of muscle showed right through that tee,
mounds rolling out into plains. Then he was up & out,
smiling & full of apologies like a boy who has to be home
before midnight. He had this thing with his lover.
They could sleep around but they couldn't stay the night. Then
one night we became more than sex. That's what he said, anyway.

*

I say "anyway" because way past witching hour
one night at some swanky party I told a pretty boy about my guy.
The trees in Central Park were twisting

behind Pretty Boy—in the dark, in a window.
Pretty Boy says, "Yeah, I think I know
the guy you're talking about."

"Yeah?" "Yeah," he says, "but his lover's been gone
a long time." I don't say nothing,
not a word. But Pretty Boy?
He can't shut his trap any more than a dog
leashed to a parking meter while its master shops.
"You know, gone

as in *dead* and gone. Gone as in six feet under."
Don't get me wrong. I don't believe everything I hear,
especially not when it's coming from a pretty boy downing 'em
like a Venus Flytrap with a glass full of live ones.
And I, well, I've had a few myself.
Still and all, I gotta say

we did go at each other—my guy & me—
like two men on the run,
like angry mixed with sad
mixed with no regrets.
Hoping, maybe. Hoping
the more friction (fiction?) we made,

the more we'd keep it away,
the way my cat kept away.
He'd been scared, that cat, flared-tail scared
he'd get the heel of my leg
or the back of my guy's palm.
Or maybe with all that was black

& all that was blue
between guys like him

& me, maybe we figured,
"What's a little more black,
what's a little more blue?"
Like fireflies—they don't ask why

they're circling over the markers,
burning themselves out
after a downfall. They just do.

Old Friend

You were sitting, looking
lost & disheveled, slice
of pizza half-eaten
before you. It wasn't wrong—
was it?—to ask you back
from Ray's on 7th,

to be glad to have you
alone for once, you who'd been
the sweet quiet activist,
the one who hung back
when the rest of us took
to chanting, chanting

& sign-wielding in the streets:
AIDSGATE; SILENCE = DEATH.
It was wrong—& what would
our old chanting, sign-wielding
friends say?—since, yes,
if you'd said yes, I would have

had you there, on my bed,
where you, of course, gave
nothing of yourself
& dementia was taking
any part of you that wasn't
nailed down: "Used to be,"

you rambled on, "I could have
any man I wanted—
you know?—any man. *Do*

you know what I mean? No,
I don't suppose *you* would."
It's not that you weren't right—

only that cruelty fit you
poorly as your skin did,
beginning, as it was, to sag
under the weight
of it, all of it.
What a cruelty in you.

what a cruelty in me—
it wouldn't let us
forget your beauty.

Club St. Vitus Male Dancer

St. Vitus, patron of epileptics, dancers, a protector
against storms. . . . Legend has it that though the
Romans tortured Vitus for his Christianity, he
emerged unscathed & was guided back home by an
angel.

I dance because many can't.
I dance because so many can.

Dance because I pass for white
but my soul is black

& black is what my earthly angel daddies wore,
black's what my earthly angel daddies wore for over twenty years.

They wore it on the sleeves, the venous sleeves of their hearts,
& it wore them.

They reined it, reined sadness in strobing, blood-lit chambers,
& sadness reined them.

Do you feel the pounding?
See their arms raised high?

Disease can't stop me. I dance.
Some would love to hurt me; I dance.

Dance to forget
what my sweet angel daddies told me to remember.

Dance to remember
what they told me to forget.

Lullaby

I've got half a mind for the rain,
Half for the sun that pins it up in steamy curls.
Or is it half for the hissing heat,
Half for the epic bleat
Of the far, faraway sheep?

Have you half a mind
To hit your cozy nest?
Half a mind to give it a rest?
There-there, pretty daddy, give it a rest.

The quarter, then the full moon
Comes so soon.
Have half a mind for the deep,
Half a mind to sink in sleep.

I've got half a mind to rock you, daddy,
& half a mind to rock you.

Across a Table

"I'm glad you're positive."
"I'm glad you're positive,

too, though, of course, I wish
you weren't." *I wish you weren't*

either is the response I expect.
But you say nothing.

And who can blame you?
Not me. I'm not the one

who'll call you after dinner and a movie.
You're not the one who'll call me.

We both know we have
that—what?—that ultimate date

one night to come, one bright morning.
Who can blame us? Not the forks

and not the knives that carry on
and do the heavy lifting now.

Your Wish

To see some of the 21st
was your wish—a wish so ambitious for its time it went
unfulfilled. And who were *you*? I can't remember
exactly—just one of the handsome—
or not—whose demise I learned of not long after
you stopped showing up Monday through Friday for hot lunch

& a shoulder to rage on. No lunch
today. Instead: just this taste of what comes first
in 2004 (since just a taste is what you were last after):
thanks to the cell & satellite, private conversation has gone
the way of the dinosaur & the horse-drawn hansom.
No one seems to remember

what it's like to be alone, at least not the way you remember
being alone—sweaty sheets, cracks in the ceiling. . . . We get to
        the airport early, lunch
low-fat, low-carb, low-sugar. The quest for the handsome
figure goes on & many of us have gone
on, assumed there is a global warming (not the first
in Time, but clearly the first man-made). After

one hot day comes the next. Then a cold change. After-
ward it starts all over again: summer, spring. . . . I can remember
amateur philosophies like that one, but your name—it's gone
from my information highway. At work I eat lunch
& surf the Web, check my e-mail first
& last for love. Through the window I can see something like a
        horse-drawn hansom

being drawn by something like a country horse as they go
their rounds of Central Park. The riders get off & pay. We pay &
    pay. . . . You came first,
whatever your name was, & you, I forget to remember,
died faster, suffered more, despite the hot lunches.
All this may or may not be what you want

to hear. So, although you're air, thin air, gone & went,
I'll end with Hubble, which did send back some handsome
pix—more colorful than a well-balanced lunch—
sightsome sights of the pinwheel & the spiral glow that came
    after
the Big Bang & forced us to remember
we were far from first,

don't know what comes after,
even the handsome are not remembered
& breakfast, lunch & dinner still come first.

Testing Positive

The universe at times is simply that which lies
above—often a naked lightbulb disturbs.
Larvae make their earth in a chest of blond-
wood drawers; winter breaks, and a sweater
slips over me—a fabric thin with holes.
Above me, men's eyes have starred open,
collapsed to seism. The universe when they rolled
off me became cliché, became cracked ceiling.

Why fear my rise to the water-stain peel of death?
Today I watched an old man in a barber's chair.
His universe was the woman who, mortician-like,
clipped, circled, the drag of her feet sweeping hair,
her breath and comb caterpillars on his face
and how she trimmed his eyebrows with great care.

That Big Noise

Dawn—and not God?—wedges a space, opens a door to another day. And in that moment, for less than a moment, you hear yourself—snoring!—and feel betrayed. You think: That big noise I keep down all day lets itself out? That big noise—the one that lets itself be seen, that lets itself be heard only in the liquid motion of eyes—that noise has a lot to say: I bring a cargo, it drones, of food and drink; I bring this bloody thing I've hurt, but look!, it growls and whines, it's still alive. In this snort, this whistle and lip-smack, everything I've ever read, seen, heard . . . is reaching up, an om-like chant.

Before you can go on too much longer, the pillow would, if it could, tell you to shut up, to get up and get ready. No one's listening, it would say and, besides, I've soaked it all up—babe, I've soaked it all up.

Driving to Lake Superior

for Rick and Tony

A fire burned here.
Black—lifeless?—a stand of trees
   holds its position.

A ghost regiment
      demanding reparation?
Let memory stand.

We start the car, move
      on. It's not empty—this threat—
their stand to our stand.

                    ***

Under a blue sky,
      three men drive toward a blue
sky, sky all around.

      It's said you can't hide,
not from God. This must be what
      that means, this blue dome

sky. Though clouds gather
      now. And now it rains. Heaven
cools its flame-blue burn.

II

Revenant Image

Image I've tried many times
in many failed poems, unsure
of what it meant—now it speaks
clearly. Now it says, *what you see*
is the scale balanced: Two square patches
of green divided by a strip of cement.
Old woman in one patch, clipping;
young man in the other, mowing.
And now it speaks of other images:
most days the boy lay sprawled

across the couch, engrossed in a novel
yellowing with taboo and hidden
by the cover of a larger novel.
Most days she lived reproaching him
for what he'd done or what he hadn't.
But days they took to the yard
he heaved and sweated, content to mow.
She said little on her knees, clipping
and clipping. Their matted dog panted so
you would have sworn it was smiling.

Pecking Orders

Here one rooster and two hens
leave a trail in sand some truant
wind will lift. My eyes, once
green and globed as a grape,
fade to hazel, flatten to gray:

plucking a handful of fruit,
what a cool relief that was
in the wavering air of this small town.
Sand dripped from my scalp,
drizzled from the dry ford of my ear.

And when a grape seemed too young,
I stood on tiptoe and balanced it
high on a refrigerator shelf
sure that Father's twin sisters
would eat it. They always did.

His sisters, they said Father
was handsome, that he never
drank his green eyes red,
never beat his wife. They said
he pushed her around a little,

the way their father did their mother,
a little. High noon again and again
I rise, waiting for the cloud
who would lift me
in her dark and purpled arms.

Sissy Boy

When they first came, panting, begging
at back doors, grandparents laid out
scraps of food. Grandchildren stroked
a thin flank, a small, trembling spine.
And they remained, nameless,
but fattened and multiplied.

They took to running in packs that barked
and turned the whole block in its sleep.

One boy dreams hunger, poison
hissing. He rolls off the bed.
A breath escapes in a rush across linoleum.

His own mother made the call.
Whining, baying, they struggled,
but they were nothing more than strays,
a haze of bristle and fur,
to be netted, caged.

Now the streets lay quiet, no howling
or mating. Trampled gardens unfurl.
Trash cans brim their empties.
And mamacitas—they sigh,
content without the sound of a wanton dog
defending itself in the middle of night,
fending off the fickle pack that turns on it,
the whimpering of the weak-haunched.

Now

One eye reads "Born then," the other "Dead now"—
Between them I'm alive, I'm dead some time now.

O'Hara & Crane won't grace the lectern today.
I'd sell my jaundice-eared volumes for a dime now.

The price of getting some? It's gone presidential.
Deceit, petty theft—*my* little crimes now.

You won't kiss? Refuse any kind of condom?
You'll do. Please do. We're falling, falling to rhyme now.

Damn the young he-beauties, they tigerwalk
On what might have been my prime. Now

God's voice comes, goes like the last, the next high:
"Steven, come, come—the sublime's now."

Punched

A fist is coming at you, fast as love
and yet slowly, too, *in* slow-motion, slow
as love. This man who's thrown his weight at you loves
his drink—my God, his breath!—and then he'd just love
everyone out of his way. He is it: that face-to-face
every subway rider dreads, counts, recounts. Still, love
of your city will bring you back to this unloved
station. You can't live like a shut-in.
God knows: you already live too deep inside
your head, wondering, in better moments, about love,
the universal, the personal. But, to return to the punch,
you're falling, propelled by the punch

as by the weight of your backpack. Punched,
you've been punched in the face, your first time. Love
was never like this. I mean, your father punched
his many wives. But you're nothing like him. You don't punch
a woman because she's too slow
already with the dinner. You've never punched
anyone. Now you're on the other side of a punch,
spinning in the air, past five, six stairs, saving face
by somehow landing on your feet. Quickly, and slowly,
it comes to you: you want to punch
him back, a hook to the jaw, a jab to the chin.
Fuck turning the other cheek. But now you're safe inside

the R that just rolled in instead
and as if she'd fallen punch-drunk
for you—my God, her perfume!—a woman is clinging
to you. That man back there, was he insane
besides being drunk? Jesus, for love
or money she'll never understand why instead
of just saying "excuse me" he sent you into

the air that way! And if only the train were slower,
quieter, you and this woman, you could take it slow,
figure out what just happened. Instead
you both grow quiet. You turn and face
the rattling window where your face,

reflected, trembles like your hands; your face
which doesn't hurt as much you might think—
it's just the shock, and that your face
is your mother's and, deeper in, your father's face,
which you've always dreamed of punching.
Tonight you'll gasp and that dream will surface
like a diver breaching from some amniotic fluid only to face
the heat of another day. For now, you'd love
to talk, and no, not about love,
or anything that foolish. But the woman and her face

are growing smaller on wheels that spark, slowly
disappearing into the tunnel. And you are slowly
mounting the stairs to the street where nothing is slow
except the old, infirm, and homeless, their faces—
some of them, you think—like your attacker's. Slowly
you're putting together the story of why your face—
your upper lip—is swollen. You will tell it—slowly
or quickly, as circumstances allow—to friends in
restaurants and strangers in bars—and in
some eyes, it will incriminate you—until slowly
you grow tired of it, the way love
grows old and you say I don't love

him. But it's a lie, rote as anyone's love
for his father, drunk in slow.
So go home, undress, and wash your face.
Come morning, you'll wake and somewhere—deep within
the mirror's eye—he'll lift your face, say, "You were punched."

The Next Right Thing

Be faithful to the morning diary entry—that date, of sorts, with yourself—to start-time 9:00 a.m., the appointment with the doctor's cold scope at noon. Say goodbye. Say hello. Be faithful to each one, one by one. And in your dreams at night, you'll be a bigger infidel. To begin, you're in the home you've made for yourself. Then, without so much as a kiss to all you've made, with nothing but the rapid movement of an eye, you're in a home others made for you. And though you're not a child anymore, everything will be as it was when you were five, or nine. The rocking chair piled high with your mother's clothes. The living room floor trafficked by your brother's toy cars. Then, more movement, and you're in a place you've never been; a place you didn't plan to go; but a place you did buy the ticket to. With dreams—you're in luck—it's a round-trip. Awake again, recount out loud the dream that philanders between present, past, and future. Or write it down. Or it will leave you. Awake again, attend to something all too real, the need to pee, to expel what, for such a short time, was yours and yours alone.

Have You Heard the One about the Chicken and the Egg Having Sex?

A chicken and an egg are having sex;
the chicken feathery, even on his back,
but with no self-consciousness about the feathers;
the egg smooth with not one sign of the nick
that betrays the razor, the stubble
that suggests the kiss of wax.

Chicken may wish Egg laughed at his jokes,
his awkward, awkward clucking,
that Egg did not just lie there rolling from side
to side, though its rolling is so vulnerable—
what, with no arms to stop itself, no wings to flap—
and its rolling may be the motion if not the sound

of laughter. Egg, for its part, is grateful.
Chicken does not comment
on its—the egg's—indeterminate sex
which—Egg is no fool—may just be a man
getting what he can, where he can and when.
But, then, there are worse things than being needy.
Who knows this better than one
who must be sat on? Chicken flutters

from the sand bed and walks away clucking something
under his breath. Egg, unbroken, but broken, lies there,
says nothing, knowing Chicken will be back,
not caring, for now, which came first.

Ms. Daydream to You

To be read aloud
in a woman's voice
with a Russian accent.

Of him much is written; little of Me—Me,
the Daydream.
      Mr. Dream, ha!, he must live
with the brouhaha of the psychobabble paparazzi
while I am free to walk to the streets with less . . . pizzazz.
Does your therapist ask you please
to write down your daydreams?
No, he does not.
      No matter. I am there
when you shake the handsome stranger's hand,
when you cut open the patient's gut. . . .

Little of what I put in your head comes true.
But what do you want? I am a full-bodied
voluptuous woman, but I can work
only with what I have to work.
I guess that I—Ms. Daydream—I am like life.
I am a bitch. But I feel very close to you
in your "disappointments." You can forgive

if all this is confusing, bizarre?
It is how I work, my charm.
Oh, please to offer me a cigarette?

[You light the match. Ms. Daydream leans in, then exhales.]

Rebuke me, my darling, and you rebuke yourself—
that much I have in common with big-shot Mr. Dream.

43

Two Nocturnes

Not a sound from him.
It's all her. All moans and breath,
And though the bit
of sky my window lets me have
tonight has no moon,
I don't mind being woken, feel no embarrassment.
Jealousy doesn't light
the dark room green. She quiets down now and then.
"They're finally falling," I tell
the cats, "to sleep." But there she is again.
Moans. Breaths.
The poor suffering springs.
Where does she go
moments we hear nothing from her?
Does she travel far? Or merge
with him as night with day at dawn? For once
I don't have to have
the answer. I tug the sheets and roll back to sleep.

*

A web grows between the pane
and the window-guard. "Grows"
because I haven't actually seen the spider.
So it's as though the web sprouts
as a flower sprouts. As though the stealthy
spider *is* a seed. "Flower," although
the web is not elegant or architectural,
ziggurat-like in its progression upward.
It's ramshackle, unselfconscious.
I ask myself how far I'll let this go.

New Love

She was the one who walked the dog—
his dog. And one day two weeks ago,
their front door as open as their faces, they worked
on their place, putting out what they didn't want
anymore: knickknacks, outgrown clothes,
a few pieces of sagging wicker furniture.
Rummaging through their discards, 3B
went on about how nice it was—

wasn't it?!—that Ron had such a nice fiancée.
How could I feel comfortable, after that, after all
that, kissing Simon in the hall the night
we'd heard them through the wall—
"You're a sick fuck! Get your shit and get out!"—
when kissing him felt something like victory?

Poem for a Friend Troubled by Noise

Your neighbors are irritants, I know—reminders
of regrets, of resolves forgotten: every drag
of their dresser drawers the drag and exhalation
of a cigarette some rude stranger smokes
in a public place he shouldn't—
you cast a sidelong glare but never say a word;
every thump of a chair-leg against their hardwood floor
the thump of the bed when X gave it to you good, so good
with so many kind words in the dark-afterward—
X—whom you never heard from again;
every tremulous moment of quiet adding up
to the moments dread builds,
moments that sometimes, admit it, end
in a quiet you don't bargain for—O unlucky you.
If that is all that bothers you, as long as you ask me
again, I say let them go on breaking
your heart, slamming the door to theirs
in your face, waking you before sunrise.

Meditations on Three Men

How he washed only the sheets that day. How on his knees by
the closet he said, "There's something pure about washing
only the sheets."

How our sleeping & our waking gave & gave the illusion of a
series of beginnings & ends to what had no end until it
ended.

How I hadn't spoken that language for years & by saying
nothing to a man I learned to lie & lie in it again.

How we police the edges—hair-cutting, fingernail-clipping. . . .
Or how it all gets away from us, how the border-sign
fades, becomes illegible.

How afterward he was dressing. N. padded out of the closet, M.
not far behind. How he said, "The cats, they're
reemerging." And how you loved him.

How I've heard that when lightning strikes in a dream, it's
preparation for one or more forks in waking time. How
everything isn't true. How lightning is.

How somewhere one thing is always eclipsing another, body
passing between sun and planet, dream between him &
him & him.

In Your Defense

A TV jingle makes its tinny way into your recurring dream,
proof that dreams are not so strong as some would have
it. A mere "no" falling from a set of lips, a rejection in the
form of a form letter, have forced many a dream to wake
and smell the coffee. And do you see? Already you've
confused night- with daydream, fantasy with exaggeration.
This, in your defense, is a common error. He said, "What
a nightmare!" And he didn't mean that he'd just returned
from sleep. He meant that on his way to you he stood, and
was jostled on a crowded underground car.

If it sounds as though you're down on dreams—or him—
you aren't and you are. With dreams we can be in two
places. Your cat naps. She is in your bed meowing a muted
meow—some dream-version of you, maybe, snatches her
latest precious plaything away. She twitches but can't shake
herself to consciousness—some dream-bird she wants
to kill escapes. (Easier—isn't it?—to say "cat" when you
meant once he was in your bed—and spoke to another in
his sleep. To say "kill," when you meant love.)

A good day can be dreamlike. You think, "I'll wake and
ruin this." But you don't wake. You fall to sleep. Later—
months, years, it won't matter because it will seem a
lifetime—you'll wake. A cold room, just you, the cat. The
music will play like an insult, yesterday's soundtrack.
You'll throw back the sheets, wipe your mouth, switch
it off.

At the North Sea

Naaktstrand

It wasn't your nakedness—
I've seen you naked many times—
but your nakedness in beach-light
that distinguished the moments
you led me up a sand hill, down
to the grass dunes where we made love.

Just what stood out
in that light overcast by clouds
I'm not sure, maybe the way
the hair on your legs, blond at sunrise,
had seemingly grown darker,
your tan skin paler.

We're subjects of locale
and light, any combination
of forces bigger than ourselves—
I suppose that's what I'm getting at.
So that when you arched toward me,
your navel, more than just your navel,

was the pink underside of a shell,
stripped of whatever it once held,
or the molten innards of a planet.
It was easy, then, to picture us from above:
two infinitesimal phenomena crawling
on, rolling over and around each other.

The universe is expanding
or contracting. Black holes are the beginning
and sometimes the end of galaxies. Everything
is spinning. But in that all-engulfing view
there was nothing cold or diminishing,
nothing that dwarfed us.

Meditations on the Jordaan

How you stirred & said, "Hold me," & holding you I imagined it
was me pulling you through your tunnel of that day's
dreams.

How I assured you, "I wrote down those lines before I forgot."
How, mouth full of sleep, you answered, "Poor little birds,
trapped in paper cages."

How you looked up & said, "Tell me again how long you're
here," & it had nothing to do with T-cells or hospital beds.
Everything with our bed.

How you tried to teach me the long *o*, the short *e* of your name.
How they were too short, too long too little a time on my
tongue.

How every morning the peal of bicycle bells, the sigh of the
tram. The sound & shadow of a bird's wings flapping the
morning we fought.

How you pedaled me past the Eerste Looiersdwarsstraat, right &
east past three, four canals, left at the Singel.

How two days before departure there were three petals scattered
about, two wilted flowers in the vase. One in full bloom.

Lovely Thought

The abbé knows this as one knows things
in dreams without having learned them.

—JEAN GENET

Lovely thought: that thought from *Our Lady of the Flowers*: that knowledge comes in dreams. (As it seems to come from nowhere else.) Knowledge. Of where love is. Of how others see the dreamer. Oh, and the why. The wind. The next ice age. And another lovely: "a light seen only in dreams." A bright light? The light of knowledge? That same knowledge that can be as much a prison as a prison? *Our Lady* doesn't say. Could it be dream-knowledge is merciful? That—like the knowledge that comes with intoxication—it doesn't stick? So that when the alarm rings, it's just a clock going off again unerringly beside the dreamer's bed.

Postcard from Ground Level

The man with the walker I've met once before
        informs me my Sunday load
would be easier if I tossed

        my laundry bag
down, met it at the next landing,
        kicked it or tossed it again & so on

until I reach ground level. He's curmudgeonly—
        God, has he always dressed like that
or was it 9/11?—

        with eyes blue & clear as any American
dream nested beneath the fierce eagle
        stitched to his trucker's hat.

So I try his strategy—
        try, even, to see myself as a hulking Greek athlete—
gleaming wrestler, naked javelin thrower—

        then quickly abandon the fantasy
& the strategy. It's violent. And besides, balancing
        my own work-wear—breathing—step

by step is good for the legs.
        (You love my legs.)
Now I'm waving "thanks"

        to the handsome Indian couple who just pointed
to the gray dress pants
        that seem to have taken a walk

from the big red cart I'm pulling across Stratford.
　　　I'm thinking what it might have been like
to find them—my pants—spot them

　　　getting good & wind-slapped, pockets full of nothing.
Like finding myself on my own way back?
　　　Lady-fainted from fatigue? Half a man?

　　　　　　　　　　　　　　　　I miss you

& miss you most on days like this
　　　when if it's not laundry that needs doing,
then it's groceries:

　　　cans of cranapple, split-pea soup, eggs
& my own incessant hunger straining my arms.
　　　Two means twice the load

but twice the endurance, even on a bad day
　　　with you, the two of us
at each other's throats.

　　　There's Old Man Stars & Stripes again,
about to begin his slow, assisted rise
　　　to the top. It's night where you climb your stairs

& you still can't believe it: you can't live
　　　in the States because you're foreign-born
& HIV-positive. It's day where I climb & I can, I do

　　　believe it.
　　　　　　"After you?" I say.
"*No.*" Old Man Stars & Stripes extends
　　　a strong & elegant arm, "*After you.*"

Scene of the Accident

The little dream is dying. Give him some space, would you? He did all he could, this little dream, to make himself a blueprint for Master's actions. He egged Master on to the initial approach. Initial, approach—big words for such a little dream. And what if Little Dream plays dumb, pretending not to know how big a dream he really is? What if little dreams fool themselves, fool their masters, too? The point is, he did it. He took Master beyond the initial approach to that first kiss, a first kiss that was, in this case, the last & unrequited kiss. Now Master's angry. (As if dreams didn't fail all the time!) Now Master's coming on like a Mack truck. And so the little dream is dying. See how he wags his tail at his master's sudden return to tenderness. See his floppy little sex gone belly up. Stand back! Give him some space, would you? Give the little guy some space.

The Last AIDS Cat

Steve's cat Harley may be the last AIDS cat.
The dying John entrusted Harley to Steve & Roger
& Harley has lived ten-plus years in the two
men's trust, then just Steve's trust.

When he wasn't sleeping through the days
of Steve & Roger, Harley followed the flows
& ebbs of love—the way each morning he follows
& pads after ever-smaller puddles

of water in the drying bathtub—
until there's nothing left to lap
but the memory of quivering cool water
on a summer day, New York. . . .

Steve's cat Harley recently went blind.
Like most Americans he is living longer,
costing more. Steve must administer
expensive meds, which make Harley's shit stink.

But he—Harley—is the same mellow cat
he always has been. What choice did he have
but to accept changing masters,
break-ups & steamy reunions?

Steve is in the shower just now.
I am sitting on his couch, half-dressed,
flipping through a coffee-table book
heavy with pornography of the past.

This page is a panoramic, 19th century. Left to right,
there are men & women, penetration: vaginal
& oral; gay & straight—really quite exciting.
Harley is suddenly standing in the middle of the room,

his black-on-white coat no longer as interesting
as the tear-pooled eyes,
the large head atop the thinning body.
The last AIDS cat is nosing about,

sniffing the air in that way cats have.
"Harley," I say, tapping the ground—
& Harley, having forgotten I am here—
looks as though he's seen a fucking ghost.

At the Delacorte

Two swans: the swan
    on the lake   and the swan reflected
on the surface of. . . .   Shall we call it Swan Lake?

    Two theaters: the theater on Swan Lake
and, on its shore,   an outdoor theater
    host this evening   to a play *in medias res.*

All this doubling!   It has me believing
    I can see one actor   standing on the stage
and the same actor   reflected on its surface,

    the actor's "real" character   standing,
fictional character   reflected.
    I'm not sure   what I'm saying

except that since yesterday   I've been unable to move
    the left side of my face—   it's nothing,
a mild case   of Bell's Palsy,

    not HIV-related.   My penchant for frowning
and grinning will live again.   Ignorant for now
    and at the Delacorte   I'm doubled too:

I sit calmly   watching *Measure*
    for Measure. I tremble   inside myself
as the reflection of the swan   on Swan Lake must tremble

    in the wings.   I bargain with God.
And I refuse   to compromise. *If You make me*
    all right,   *I swear I'll never. . . .*

Oh, to hell   with You.
    Bored, the swans   fly east
until, that is, the swans above   the water, in the air,

    flaps past the grimy border   of Swan Lake
and the reflected swan's   no more.
    No. Now there's just   the one.

At Macondo

Mornings I soaked in the shade
of a giant oak and gave of myself
to the two-winged Culicidae.
You might even say the mosquito
had a drink—*a bloody Mary, say*—

on me, that she drank *of* me.
Anyway, it seemed fair trade
for a peaceful place to rest
my bones, change in my pocket,
work far off. I could spend

every morning just this way:
the song of the early bird,
the muddy rhythm of the frogs
who'd carried on all night.
One who sang to me never did

show his face (green and thick?).
I swiveled east, spun west
only to find him hiding, shy
and afraid I wouldn't love him.
You know I would have kissed him.

You know I would have.